ECPE MICHIGAN PROFICIENCY PRACTICE TESTS FOR SUCCESS ON THE FINAL GCVR EXAM: GRAMMAR, CLOZE, VOCABULARY & READING

The Examination for the Certificate of Proficiency in English and ECPE are trademarks of the University of Michigan, in conjunction with Cambridge Assessment English, which are neither affiliated with nor endorse this publication.

ECPE Michigan Proficiency Practice Tests for Success on the Final GCVR Exam: Grammar, Cloze, Vocabulary, and Reading

© COPYRIGHT 1995, 2019 Academic Success Group dba www.michigan-test.com

All rights reserved. No part of this publication may be reproduced, stored in a retrieval system, or transmitted, in any form or by any means, electronic, mechanical, photocopying, recording, or otherwise, without the prior written permission of the copyright owner.

ISBN-13: 978-1-949282-45-0

For information on bulk discounts, please contact us at: info@michigan-test.com

NOTE: The Examination for the Certificate of Proficiency in English and ECPE are trademarks of the University of Michigan, in conjunction with Cambridge Assessment English, which are neither affiliated with nor endorse this publication.

COPYRIGHT NOTICE TO EDUCATORS

Please respect copyright law. Under no circumstances may you make copies of these materials for distribution to or use by students. Should you wish to use the materials with students, you are required to purchase a copy of this publication for each of your students.

TABLE OF CONTENTS

ECPE PRACTICE TEST 1

Grammar	1
Cloze	10
Vocabulary	12
Reading	20

ECPE PRACTICE TEST 2

Grammar	30
Cloze	38
Vocabulary	40
Reading	48

ECPE PRACTICE TEST 3

Grammar	58
Cloze	67
Vocabulary	69
Reading	78

ECPE PRACTICE TEST 4

Grammar	86
Cloze	95
Vocabulary	97
Reading	105

ANSWER KEY — 114

ECPE PRACTICE TEST 1

GRAMMAR

1. John is so shy that very rarely _____ to anyone.
   A. he speaks
   B. he is speaking
   C. does he speak
   D. he does speak

2. I bought one of those _____ books at the mall today.
   A. good $5 paperback
   B. paperback good $5
   C. $5 good paperback
   D. good paperback $5

3. The compact disks are in the cabinet _____ the CD player.
   A. that is kept
   B. which is kept
   C. where we keep
   D. kept in that

4. We want to start our business soon but right now we're sizing _____ the competition.
   A. in
   B. under
   C. up
   D. over

5. We hope _____ on our vacation on Saturday.
    A. to go
    B. to going
    C. going
    D. to have been going

6. No sooner _____ at the party than she came in.
    A. we arrived
    B. we had arrived
    C. had we arrived
    D. we were arriving

7. Alison is at home recovering _____ the flu.
    A. with
    B. to
    C. for
    D. from

8. - How did you like the show?
    - I have never seen _____ performance.
    A. such an awful
    B. so an awful
    C. such awful a
    D. a so awful

9. The police have reported that the ringleader of the gang turned _____ his conspirators.
    A. down
    B. off
    C. away
    D. against

10. The weather report said that it _____ rain tomorrow.
    A. must
    B. could
    C. ought
    D. maybe

11. - Jason always insults me.
    - Don't worry. He _____ too.
    A. does it for me
    B. does it to me
    C. does it me
    D. is doing it for me

12. My daughter didn't make the varsity team, and my neighbor's _____.
    A. didn't either
    B. didn't too
    C. didn't though
    D. did neither

13. It was either lie or steal, so I had to choose the _____ .
    A. least of two evils
    B. lesser of two evils
    C. less evil
    D. more or less evil

14. At 6'4" she is the _____ four sisters.
    A. tallest of the
    B. taller of her
    C. taller than her
    D. most tall of the

15. I enjoy swimming _____.
    A. in summer's time
    B. during summers
    C. in the summer
    D. summertime

16. I just heard that he is _____ with leukemia.
    A. afflicted
    B. affliction
    C. afflict
    D. the affliction

17. She always barges _____ without knocking.
    A. in
    B. around
    C. on
    D. about

18. It's cold outside, so you _____ take a coat.
    A. would rather
    B. should have
    C. had better
    D. wouldn't need to

19. He wouldn't have divorced her _____ faithful.
    A. she was
    B. had she been
    C. was she
    D. she had been

20. It's Barbara's last day of work on Friday, so we should chip _____ to buy her a farewell gift.
    A. with
    B. in
    C. together
    D. around

21. - Did you like the movie?
    - I preferred the one _____ .
    A. to which I saw last week
    B. I saw last week
    C. which last week I saw
    D. I saw it last week

22. I don't know _____ the money from the loan or not.
    A. whether got
    B. he got
    C. if he got
    D. that he got

23. Sarah told everyone my secret, but _____ we are still good friends.
    A. furthermore
    B. despite of that
    C. contrarily
    D. in spite of that

24. He is upset because he saw a bad accident that _____ this morning.
    A. was happening
    B. happened
    C. has happening
    D. happen

25. Someone once told me _____ to California in the summer.
    A. not to go
    B. not going
    C. not go
    D. if I not go

26. I requested that my friend _____ to the party.
    A. to be invited
    B. be inviting
    C. being invited
    D. be invited

27. Our online business is shutting down because we had _____ customers.
    A. shortage
    B. a shortage of
    C. shortage of
    D. the shortage of

28. _____ in reading popular novels, especially detective fiction and murder mysteries.
    A. I am interesting
    B. Interesting it is
    C. I am interested
    D. It is interesting

29. That is a machine _____ documents.
    A. by which transmits
    B. which are transmitted
    C. by which are transmitted
    D. which transmits

30. I would have bought that new car _____ more money.
   A. did I have
   B. have I have
   C. if I did have
   D. had I had

31. _____ so hard for the exam, I was really disappointed when I didn't pass.
   A. I did study
   B. Had studied
   C. Having studied
   D. Had studying

32. _____ I have my first exam today, I wanted to study enough and be prepared.
   A. While
   B. Because
   C. While having
   D. Because having

33. - I saw your boyfriend in the park last night.
   - You _____ have. He was with me all evening.
   A. mightn't
   B. shouldn't
   C. couldn't
   D. ought not to

34. If the weather were to improve, _____ would be better for everyone.
    A. that
    B. they
    C. then we
    D. then there

35. I heard he got the promotion, so _____ the hard work paid off for him.
    A. he was able doing
    B. he was able to do
    C. his ability doing
    D. his ability to do

36. I went out with that really popular guy in class last night, and _____ he asked me to go out again this coming weekend.
    A. in surprise
    B. surprisingly
    C. surprising
    D. surprised

37. In addition _____ , she also does knitting.
    A. to sew
    B. she sews
    C. to sewing
    D. she sewing

38. The neighborhood is so noisy that the people _____ here really don't like it.
    A. lived
    B. who living
    C. that living
    D. living

39. - Laura loves the opera.
    - Maria, _____ , hates it.
    A. on the other hand
    B. in the other hand
    C. on contrast
    D. on the contrast

40. My new job is going well, especially now that I have got used _____ so early.
    A. to getting up
    B. getting up
    C. to get up
    D. get up

CLOZE

This passage is about automobile assembly.

The manufacture (41) an automobile is a based on an assembly system which perpetually keeps (42) of each and every automotive fault, flaw, or defect. The (43) of the vehicle must encompass the testing of mechanical functions, (44) the implementation of automotive safety standards required by various regulatory bodies. For example, the (45) system must conform (46) the standards of the Environmental Protection Agency (EPA), which (47) the emission of noxious fumes (48) contaminate the atmosphere. In addition, the installation of air (49) and seat belts is compulsory for both the driver and passenger sides of the vehicle. The chassis of the automobile (50) must also meet certain requirements.

41. a. of   b. with   c. for   d. by
42. a. recording   b. limit   c. track   d. path
43. a. manipulation b. situation   c. defamation   d. fabrication
44. a. together   b. as well as   c. not only   d. without
45. a. course   b. device   c. exhaust   d. position
46. a. also   b. by   c. all   d. to
47. a. stop   b. impede   c. prohibit   d. hinder
48. a. indeed   b. that   c. in   d. now
49. a. bags   b. sacks   c. pockets   d. systems
50. a. oneself   b. itself   c. which   d. it

This passage is about college admission.

Many students dream of attending college and embarking (51) an exciting career. However, not every student wants to spend four years at college. A two-year program in the community college system is an (52) for these students. Community colleges have a(n) (53) enrollment policy, which means that they do not consider grade point average or placement test scores for admission. These colleges are accessible (54) anyone able to pay the tuition. The (55) of the programs these institutions offer make them attractive to students fettered (56) family or work-related responsibilities. The community college system is not (57) its drawbacks, however. One shortcoming is accommodation. On-campus housing is often not (58) for students living away from home. (59) consideration is that these institutions do not offer Bachelor of Arts degrees, (60) only Associate of Arts degrees.

51. a. for   b. on   c. at   d. in
52. a. advocate   b. incentive   c. alternate   d. option
53. a. wide   b. open   c. flexible   d. variable
54. a. with   b. for   c. about   d. to
55. a. flexibility b. malleability c. variability   d. adaptability
56. a. under   b. down   c. with   d. to
57. a. lacking   b. without   c. showing   d. with
58. a. provided   b. provincial   c. provident   d. providence
59. a. More   b. Additional   c. Another   d. Also
60. a. however   b. but   c. and   d. but also

VOCABULARY

61. Farming and raising animals are _____ activities.
    A. herbivorous
    B. carnivorous
    C. deciduous
    D. agrarian

62. The child was _____ on his chewing gum.
    A. inhaling
    B. gnawing
    C. exhaling
    D. respiring

63. There has been a very _____ change in the weather recently.
    A. profuse
    B. confined
    C. perceptible
    D. imperative

64. The painting depicts a _____ of seagulls at the seaside.
    A. unit
    B. livestock
    C. flock
    D. team

65. Dogs usually _____ their tails when they are happy and content.
    A. wag
    B. growl
    C. hatch
    D. migrate

66. People who walk around glued to their phones might as well have _____ on their eyes.
    A. hitches
    B. bridles
    C. harnesses
    D. blinders

67. Gold is a _____ that is mined underground.
    A. commodity
    B. implements
    C. fodder
    D. fumigation

68. The cruel man was _____ his dog with a wooden stick.
    A. lashing
    B. cultivating
    C. coaxing
    D. irrigating

69. Elderly people are often _____ to broken bones.
    A. sprout
    B. stout
    C. vicious
    D. prone

70. I bought these jeans at a _____ price.
    A. contrition
    B. weary
    C. bargain
    D. dingy

71. What a(n) _____ painting. Where did you buy it?
    A. superficial
    B. gorgeous
    C. facetious
    D. ostensible

72. He will spend 20 years in prison for his involvement in _____ activities.
    A. illicit
    B. genial
    C. prudent
    D. witty

73. The _____ child displayed a total lack of respect for his parents.
    A. wistful
    B. superfluous
    C. impudent
    D. earnest

74. After a year overseas, Bill _____ to see his family back home.
    A. emulated
    B. yearned
    C. deplored
    D. budged

75. Our lack of money is a(n) _____ towards finishing the project.
    A. token
    B. blandishment
    C. subsistence
    D. stumbling block

76. The pigeons were sitting on the _____ of the building.
    A. lurk
    B. lark
    C. ledge
    D. lunatic

77. In order to be a good parent, one must _____ a caring attitude.
    A. regress
    B. snub
    C. foster
    D. stifle

78. I wouldn't keep company with a(n) _____ character like him.
    A. charming
    B. unsavory
    C. timid
    D. elated

79. The situation was _____ with stress and tension.
    A. fraught
    B. manifest
    C. blue
    D. clandestine

80. The water was _____ and not fit for drinking.
    A. frivolous
    B. wayward
    C. obsequious
    D. murky

81. I couldn't _____ what she was trying to explain.
    A. jettison
    B. kindle
    C. fathom
    D. beckon

82. Our next-door neighbors _____ all night at their celebration.
    A. capitulated
    B. haunted
    C. capsized
    D. reveled

83. The forest fire was _____ by a carelessly discarded cigarette.
    A. ignited
    B. submerged
    C. retired
    D. forged

84. He went to Hollywood in _____ of becoming a famous actor.
    A. frail
    B. quest
    C. fringe
    D. gait

85. She has been so _____ since her mother died.
    A. blue
    B. ruthless
    C. green
    D. fallacious

86. A(n) _____ exists between the United States and the United Kingdom concerning such matters.
    A. debris
    B. relic
    C. jetty
    D. treaty

87. This suitcase is very _____ and should last a long time.
    A. indefatigable
    B. sturdy
    C. supercilious
    D. inimical

88. Maria was caught in a sudden _____ without her umbrella.
    A. deluge
    B. effigy
    C. ambush
    D. crevice

89. This painting _____ a battle in the Far East.
    A. strands
    B. engulfs
    C. depicts
    D. repels

90. He told us a(n) _____ story about ghosts and monsters.
    A. lush
    B. staunch
    C. jagged
    D. eerie

91. John's proposal has many _____ , although it has positive points as well.
   A. prerogatives
   B. shortcomings
   C. aspirations
   D. trends

92. There is a(n) _____ of books on the subject.
   A. congruity
   B. overabundance
   C. parameter
   D. jurisdiction

93. I find his lewd jokes to be quite _____ .
   A. eminent
   B. imminent
   C. winsome
   D. licentious

94. The car _____ over the center line, causing the accident.
   A. imposed
   B. protracted
   C. lurched
   D. enlisted

95. The mother is often awarded _____ of the children in divorce proceedings.
   A. ransom
   B. interment
   C. custody
   D. testimony

96. Jane is a(n) _____ about her exercise routine.
    A. zealot
    B. hearth
    C. rodent
    D. municipality

97. The boxer threw a _____ at his opponent.
    A. gait
    B. loot
    C. punch
    D. stumbling block

98. After hours without food or water, the children began to _____ .
    A. procrastinate
    B. stifle
    C. grumble
    D. reproach

99. Secret agents often engage in _____ .
    A. lassitude
    B. consequences
    C. subterfuge
    D. sequences

100. Don't be _____ by his false promises.
    A. lured
    B. shriveled
    C. simmered
    D. withered

READING

This passage is about a famous researcher.

Born in France in 1896, Jean Piaget went on to become one of the most influential thinkers in the areas of educational psychology and child development in the twentieth and twenty-first centuries. The primary thrust of his research revolved around the question: "How do human beings come to know?" His research culminated in the groundbreaking discovery of what he called "abstract symbolic reasoning." The basic idea behind this principle was that biology influences child development to a greater extent than does socialization. That is to say, Piaget concluded that younger children answered research questions differently than older ones not because they were less intelligent, but because their intelligence was at a lower stage of biological development.

Because he was a biologist, Piaget had a keen interest in the adaptation of organisms to their environment, and this preoccupation led to many astute observations. Piaget found that behavior in children was controlled by mental organizations called "schemes," which enable an individual to interpret his or her world and respond to situations. Piaget *coined* the term "equilibration" to describe the biological need of human beings to balance these schemes against the processes of environmental adaptation.

The French-born biologist postulated that schemes are innate since all children are born with these drives. Noting that while other animals continued to deploy their in-born schemes throughout the entire duration of their lives, Piaget hypothesized that human beings' pre-existing, innate schemes compete with and ultimately diverge from constructed schemes, which are socially-acquired in the environmental adaptation process.

As Piaget's research with children progressed, he identified four stages of cognitive development. The final developmental stage is called the formal operational stage. During this stage, the individual should be able to grasp abstract thought on a range of complex ideas and theories. Unfortunately, recent research has shown that adults in many countries around the globe have failed to complete this stage, perhaps owing to poverty or poor educational opportunities.

101. In the third sentence of paragraph 1, what does the phrase "abstract symbolic reasoning" suggest?
    A. The idea that younger children are less intelligent that older children.
    B. The idea that younger children are less physically developed than older children.
    C. The idea that younger children are less socially developed than older children.
    D. The idea that younger children are less culturally developed than older children.

102. According to the passage, what was the greatest influence on Piaget's thinking and research?
    A. Piaget's views as a biologist affected his work on child development.
    B. Piaget discovered that the child's biological development is connected to his or her mental functioning.
    C. Piaget noted that environmental factors, as well as biological factors, played a role in child development.
    D. Piaget loved children, which led him to investigate child development.

103. Which of the sentences below contains the main idea of paragraph 3?
    A. Piaget theorized that, unlike the schemes of other animals, human beings' schemes are primarily acquired in the socialization process.
    B. In contrast to other animals, human beings use their innate schemes throughout their lifetimes, rather than departing from constructed schemes.
    C. The process by which human beings acquire schemes is different than that of other animals because human beings acquire schemes during the socialization process, and these acquired schemes bifurcate from their innate schemes.
    D. Piaget noted that human beings differ from other animals since they do not rely only on in-born cognitive mechanisms.

104. In paragraph 2, what does the use of the word *coined* suggest?
    A. Piaget controlled this phenomenon.
    B. Piaget evaluated children with this trait.
    C. Piaget created the word "equilibration".
    D. Piaget realized that individuals respond to the world and interpret situations.

105. What can the reader conclude about the formal operational stage?
    A. It is the result of poor economic conditions.
    B. It has not yet been finished by many individuals around the world.
    C. It is an important global problem.
    D. It is based on complicated scientific theories.

This passage is about the first public railway.

The world's first public railway carried passengers, even though it was primarily designed to transport coal from inland mines to ports on the North Sea. Unveiled on September 27, 1825, the train had 32 open wagons and carried over 300 people. The engine that was used to power the railway vehicle was called a locomotive. The word originates from the combination of the Latin words "locus," meaning place, and "motivus" meaning "motion." It is a shortened version of the phrase "locomotive engine," which was first used in the nineteenth century to make a distinction between mobile and stationary steam engines.

The first locomotive steam engine was powered by what was termed the steam-blast technique. The chimney of the locomotive redirected the exhaust steam into the engine via a narrow pipe. In this way, the steam created a draft of air which followed after it, creating more power and speed for the engine. The train had rimmed wheels which ran atop rails that were specially designed to give the carriages a faster and smoother ride. While the small carriages could hardly be termed **commodious**, the locomotive could accelerate to 15 miles per hour, a record-breaking speed at that time.

The inventor of the locomotive, George Stephenson, subsequently revolutionized his steam engine by adding 24 further pipes. Now containing 25 tubes instead of one, Stephenson's second "iron horse" was even faster and more powerful than his first creation.

At that time, locomotives pulled a string of carriages in the direction of travel from the front of the first carriage in the string. Outside North America, the push-pull operation became increasingly common. In this setup, one locomotive pulled the carriages from the front and another locomotive pushed them from behind. The locomotive at the end of the train was controlled from a cab at the front of the train. This rear locomotive is not to be confused with a caboose, a rail transport vehicle at the end of a freight train that provides shelter for the crew.

106. Why does the author give an explanation of the origin of the word "locomotive" in the first paragraph?
    A. to emphasize the fact that the invention was the first steam engine
    B. to provide an introduction for the technical language that is used in the remainder of the passage
    C. to fit in with the style of language that was in use in the nineteenth century
    D. to begin to explain how the engine worked

107. What is the main idea of the second paragraph?
    A. The locomotive would not have functioned without the steam-blast technique.
    B. The locomotive ran well because of the way that the steam was channeled.
    C. A couple of notable design features made the locomotive run fast and smoothly.
    D. The carriages were not very large, but the train was powerful and fast.

108. Why was the second locomotive that Stephenson invented an improvement on his first?
    A. because it ran more smoothly
    B. because it contained more pipes and tubes
    C. because it could carry more passengers
    D. because it ran with greater force and speed

109. As used in the passage, what does the sentence containing the word "commodious" suggest?
    A. The trains were powerful.
    B. The carriages were uncomfortable.
    C. The carriages were not very spacious.
    D. The train was speedy.

110. From the information contained in the passage, it seems reasonable to infer which of the following?
    A. Many passengers were frightened about traveling on this new locomotive.
    B. George Stephenson's inventions laid the basic foundations for modern day public trains and railways.
    C. Profits in the coal industry increased after the invention of the locomotive.
    D. Stephenson's second locomotive carried more passengers than his first one.

This passage is about the motion picture industry.

The motion picture industry, located in the heart of Hollywood, California, produces thousands of motion pictures a year. Although the movie-making process appears effortless when the movie is released to the viewing public, the process is lengthy, time-consuming, and expensive.

The first step is to obtain the movie script, which is usually procured from the Screen Writers' Guild. Since the strength of the story can make or break the production, movies with underdeveloped plots are normally refused.

The next step is to find a producer who is capable of providing the monetary endowment via a major motion picture company for the movie's production. Companies such as Touchstone and other Disney affiliates are currently among the forerunners in the motion picture production industry.

Of course, the undertaking will not materialize without the input of a director. Actors perform under the auspices of the director, and they must refrain from doing anything that he or she prohibits. Stunt men and women are also employed to perform any tasks that would endanger the safety of the actors.

In addition, the cinematography must be considered. The CGI team is responsible for all graphic enhancements to the movies, which are rendered through computer generated imagery. The camera crew works in close cooperation with the CGI team to reproduce the agreed-upon result. Many recent 3-D movies contain some of the most amazing CGI work ever produced, which provides an example of the successful collaboration of CGI and effective camera work.

The momentous event of releasing the movie to the public follows the production process. While critics may play a small role in the popularity of the movie, its success ultimately lies with its acceptance by the movie-viewing public.

111. Which statement most accurately describes a specific aspect of movie production?
    A. The movie script must originate from the Screen Writers' Guild.
    B. Productions of stories with intricate plots will receive only minimal monetary support from the motion picture company.
    C. The producer is responsible for winning financial backing from the motion picture company.
    D. The CGI team works under the tutelage of the director.

112. Which one of the following is the responsibility of the director?
    A. to co-ordinate the camera crew and the CGI team
    B. to make all decisions concerning cinematography
    C. to determine which script will be produced
    D. to provide guidance to the actors

113. What is an aspect of the work of the CGI team?
    A. Its members must not contravene the wishes of the director.
    B. It can produce magnificent cinematographic results.
    C. It must operate independently from the camera crew.
    D. It has to assigns tasks to stunt men and women.

114. The popularity of a movie is mainly dependent on which one of the following?
    A. the opinions of critics.
    B. members of the public who watch movies.
    C. the speed of the production process.
    D. the assistance provided by the motion picture industry.

115. Why does the author mention recent 3-D movies?
    A. to illustrate cinematography
    B. to explain movie enhancements in general
    C. to describe how complicated CGI effects are produced
    D. to exemplify how CGI and camera work have been recently combined

This passage is about childhood health.

Research demonstrates that children's concentration and learning suffer when they do not have a nutritious breakfast. In response to this research, some countries have developed programs for nutritious school breakfasts and dinners, and **they** have allocated more funds to these meal programs than to welfare benefits. There remains a clear need for the government to address nutrition as one of the worst symptoms of child poverty since disadvantaged children in many areas still do not get a nourishing breakfast and the effectiveness of their education is jeopardized as a result.

Smoking also greatly damages the health of children and increases childhood mortality rates. While the government has raised the cigarette tax, thereby increasing the cost of tobacco to consumers, this has not brought about the desired result. On the contrary, it has left poor parents who smoke worse off, and their children will continue to suffer. Children's health would be better served if the government allocated funds to preventing cigarette sales to children, instead of the hefty monetary resources spent on attempting to halt cigarette smuggling and related tax evasion.

Children, particularly young adolescents, are also sickly because of the ever-increasing consumption of alcohol in this age group. One reason for the rise in children's drinking is the increase in the availability of sweetened bottled alcoholic drinks like wine coolers. These beverages make alcohol more attractive and more palatable to young people and children. Nevertheless, the government appears be in something of a quandary, perhaps wishing to speak out against major beverage manufacturing companies, and yet succumbing to lobbying by and accepting related financial support from big businesses like Anheuser-Busch.

Improving children's opportunities depends on ending child poverty and improving the health of the poorest children. While these goals are related, it would be foolish to believe that the reduction of child poverty would automatically improve children's nutrition and reduce their smoking and drinking. Re-thinking the allocation of governmental funds to nutrition and effective education and prevention about addiction are still needed in order to improve child health.

116. In paragraph 1, to what does the word *they* refer?
    A. countries that have established school breakfasts
    B. children who regularly do not receive breakfast
    C. researchers in the field of child nutrition
    D. fund-raisers for school meal programs

117. Which of the sentences best expresses the main idea of paragraph 1?
    A. The government needs to provide nourishing breakfasts to children so that they can improve their learning.
    B. It is of the utmost importance for the government to improve child poverty and child nutrition.
    C. Child poverty continues to be a grave social problem; therefore, the government should get involved.
    D. Poor nutrition is one aspect of poverty and increased government funds need to be set aside to deal with this situation.

118. Why does the author discuss smoking in paragraph 2 of the passage?
    A. to establish the link between cigarette smuggling and tax evasion
    B. to exemplify how poor parents who smoke will continue to do so
    C. to enumerate details about a government policy
    D. to expand on another aspect of poor health in children

119. According to the passage, what was the main reason for the government's increase in the cigarette tax?
    A. To reduce childhood death rates
    B. To decrease tax evasion relating to tobacco products
    C. To attempt to deter smoking, particularly by poor parents
    D. To impede cigarette smuggling

120. Based on the information in paragraph 3, what can be inferred about the government's reluctance to criticize the practices of big businesses?
    A. It is loath to lose the monetary support that large beverage companies have to offer.
    B. It realizes that there is no reason to reduce the demand for certain alcoholic drinks.
    C. It wishes to reduce its reliance on financing from lobbyists.
    D. It understands that doing so would not make alcohol less attractive to youngsters.

ECPE PRACTICE TEST 2

GRAMMAR

1. Mary's business has grown _____ leaps and bounds.
   A. under
   B. in
   C. through
   D. by

2. _____ her only once since she went away to college.
   A. I have seen
   B. Did I see
   C. Have I seen
   D. I see

3. I purchased a new _____ desk for my office today.
   A. walnut rolltop traditional
   B. traditional rolltop walnut
   C. walnut traditional rolltop's
   D. traditional walnut rolltop

4. I just can't figure _____ the last exercise in the math homework.
   A. up
   B. on
   C. at
   D. out

5. I finally _____ to buy it after I had looked at several models.
   A. to decide
   B. decided
   C. deciding
   D. had decided

6. He tells so many lies that almost nothing he says is consistent _____ reality.
   A. for
   B. with
   C. in
   D. by

7. The police interrogated all of the suspects, but each one denied _____ the car.
   A. stealing
   B. to steal
   C. to stealing
   D. to have stolen

8. The teacher didn't realize that he cheated on the exam, so he got _____ it.
   A. down on
   B. through
   C. away with
   D. up to

9. - Are you going out with her again?
   - No, I've never met _____ girl.
   A. a so boring
   B. such a boring
   C. so a boring
   D. a such boring

10. This form is compulsory; in other words, you _____ fill it in.
    A. should
    B. may
    C. must
    D. could

11. We're going to Disneyland, but my sister's children _____ .
    A. aren't too
    B. aren't though
    C. are too
    D. are though

12. Sarah has appendicitis, so she is _____ hospital.
    A. in a
    B. admitted to
    C. in the
    D. admitted

13. Iced tea on a hot summer day is one of life's _____ pleasures.
    A. greater
    B. most great
    C. greatest
    D. the greatest

14. He has been extremely ill, so the last few months _____ their toll on him.
    A. taken
    B. have taken
    C. made
    D. have made

15. You would have passed your test _____ more.
    A. had you studied
    B. if you studied
    C. you had studied
    D. would you studied

16. - Want to eat at Denny's?
    - No, I _____ eat at Perkin's.
    A. would have
    B. would rather
    C. should have
    D. had better

17. I don't really like my job, but I've decided to stick it _____ .
    A. up
    B. down
    C. out
    D. on

18. That restaurant has dishes that aren't _____ anywhere else.
    A. to be served
    B. serving
    C. served
    D. to serve

19. He said to buy the book for him _____ it cost.
    A. as much as
    B. in so much as
    C. however much
    D. so much as

20. _____ skiing, I can't really say if I like it or not.
    A. Never having tried
    B. Never had trying
    C. Never to have tried
    D. Never to try

21. She would have _____ in the accident had she not put on her seat belt.
    A. bad injury
    B. been injuring badly
    C. been badly injured
    D. to be bad injured

22. _____ students here work hard and study a lot.
    A. Almost
    B. Most of
    C. Almost of
    D. Most

23. My mother is visiting me this weekend, and she is bringing my _____ brother along with her.
    A. two year
    B. two-year-old
    C. two years
    D. two-years-old

24. I like little kids _____ well-behaved.
    A. if only they are
    B. only if they are
    C. if only are they
    D. if they only are

25. - Aren't you supposed to be in Los Angeles right now?
    - Well, to _____ a long story short, I didn't go.
    A. take
    B. make
    C. put
    D. break

26. People _____ about that scandalous story in the news.
    A. constant talk
    B. constant talking
    C. constantly to be talked
    D. are constantly talking

27. He got evicted from his apartment, but what _____ was pay his rent on time.
    A. he should do
    B. should he do
    C. he should have done
    D. he should be doing

28. I am your best friend, so you know you can count _____ me.
    A. in
    B. for
    C. on
    D. by

29. We had a good discussion and arrived at a solution that can _____ .
    A. be easy done
    B. be easily done
    C. easy to be done
    D. easily to be done

30. The professor was telling us not _____ so much time talking.
    A. spending
    B. to be spending
    C. to spending
    D. be spending

31. Although the lecture was long, _____ to pay attention.
    A. I did manage
    B. despite I managed
    C. but I managed
    D. I manage

32. The doctor advised me to do something that I never would have thought _____ .
    A. to be done
    B. to do
    C. to doing
    D. of doing

33. My dad is going to stick to his guns about the price of the car because he is really _____ to get a good price.
    A. determined fairly
    B. determined well
    C. determined quite
    D. quite determined

34. Compulsory military service isn't required in our country _____ .
    A. anymore
    B. anyway
    C. anyhow
    D. anytime

35. - I think we should give him a break.
    - Why _____ that?
    A. we should do
    B. we should to do
    C. should we do
    D. should we to do

36. Other _____ idle gossip, we had absolutely nothing to talk about.
    A. from
    B. when
    C. that
    D. than

37. It's high time he _____ the situation.
    A. accept
    B. accepted
    C. accepts
    D. accepting

38. She is _____ able to park the car without hitting the curb.
    A. ever hardly
    B. never hardly
    C. hardly ever
    D. hardly never

39. - Debbie has been in such a bad mood lately that she's just unbearable.
    - Yeah, _____ bad tempered she is!
    A. how
    B. that
    C. which
    D. what

40. The store was in ruins after the break-in yesterday, and they _____ rebuild everything.
    A. will have had
    B. will have to
    C. will have had to
    D. have had

CLOZE

This passage is about political office.

Running for political office is exceptionally arduous and should not be undertaken by the (41) hearted. The candidate must first speak at local venues, where he or she endeavors to (42) the votes of his or her constituents. Any new candidates are the opponents (43) the incumbent, the person currently in office who is running for re-election. The candidates strive to (44) protocol and refrain from actions that might create animosity (45) themselves and the public. The public will be curious about, if not (46) of, the candidate's professional life, in addition to his or her personal life, which will be under (47) scrutiny during the campaign. Since his or her private life becomes public domain, the candidate may (48) to disclose any controversial behavior in his or her past before the media uncovers it. (49) history has shown us, a politician who is caught in a scandal might even be subjected (50) censure from his political colleagues.

41.	a. faint	b. meek	c. mild	d. weak
42.	a. extract	b. gain	c. exist	d. drop
43.	a. with	b. to	c. for	d. of
44.	a. observance	b. observe	c. appeal	d. appellation
45.	a. by	b. beside	c. between	d. to
46.	a. adventurous	b. dangerous	c. querulous	d. suspicious
47.	a. near	b. care	c. close	d. front
48.	a. to fit	b. see fit	c. look fit	d. be fit
49.	a. Contrary	b. Despite	c. As	d. Where
50.	a. by	b. under	c. to	d. with

This passage is about crime.

Not only is the (51) of crime rising recently, but the types of crime have also started to proliferate. Of course, the most serious crime is murder. Methods of homicide might include shooting, stabbing victims (52) a knife or sharp object, or strangling and smothering. (53) murder is even more heinous because it is deliberated and planned. Alleged assailants may become fugitives running from the law and should be (54) armed and dangerous. Members of the public are therefore advised to exercise (55) caution if encountering these individuals. Unfortunately, many crimes are drug-related. In addition to a prison sentence, (56) narcotics dealers may have to perform community service in drug rehabilitation centers, which (57) part of their punishments. Financial crimes are also growing, often resulting in large (58) losses. White-collar crimes by employees include embezzling, as well as other infringements (59) financial regulations. However, not all financial crimes are committed by employees. Notorious for exploiting the weak and vulnerable, swindlers sometimes convince their prey to invest in (60) companies.

51. a. amount   b. number   c. total   d. statistics
52. a. by   b. on   c. with   d. at
53. a. Premeditating b. Preconditioned   c. Premeditated   d. Mediation
54. a. considered   b. commenced   c. considerably   d. concerned
55. a. extreme   b. viable   c. exceptional   d. unusual
56. a. defended   b. convicted   c. declining   d. convincing
57. a. makes   b. builds   c. forms   d. works
58. a. money   b. monetary   c. monument   d. momentary
59. a. in   b. at   c. within   d. of
60. a. fiction   b. fictitious   c. artificial   d. unreal

VOCABULARY

61. He sat at the bar drinking beer from a large _____ .
    A. cork
    B. muffin
    C. larder
    D. tankard

62. You've gotten a little _____ lately. Maybe you should go on a diet.
    A. plump
    B. withered
    C. shriveled
    D. scant

63. Remove the _____ from those potatoes before boiling them.
    A. pulp
    B. strips
    C. peelings
    D. outsides

64. People with heart problems should _____ fatty food.
    A. jot down
    B. concentrate
    C. steer clear of
    D. peruse

65. Good health is _____ to living a long life.
    A. stale
    B. putrid
    C. dense
    D. vital

66. The garbage was giving off a horrible _____ .
   A. garnish
   B. morsel
   C. stench
   D. flap

67. Only a(n) _____ of the class passed the examination.
   A. concoction
   B. receptacle
   C. texture
   D. fraction

68. He _____ through his drawers, looking for his wallet.
   A. rummaged
   B. tackled
   C. simmered
   D. entailed

69. The wine was stored in a large wooden _____ .
   A. jigger
   B. cask
   C. lather
   D. stack

70. Sally's room was such a mess. I have never seen anything so totally _____ .
   A. impeccable
   B. cluttered
   C. immaculate
   D. sumptuous

71. The _____ details of the plan were known to only a few members of the group.
    A. tantamount
    B. terse
    C. loquacious
    D. covert

72. Tony always remains calm. He is _____ even under stress.
    A. apposite
    B. unanimous
    C. phlegmatic
    D. magnanimous

73. Senator Smith is the _____ seeking re-election.
    A. incumbent
    B. protocol
    C. constituent
    D. coup

74. The old building _____ with the help of explosives.
    A. purged
    B. replete
    C. jeered
    D. toppled

75. That decision can be reached only by group _____ .
    A. consensus
    B. inauguration
    C. sinecure
    D. animosity

76. The athlete had to _____ his world record title when it was discovered that he has taken drugs.
    A. endeavor
    B. banish
    C. relinquish
    D. nominate

77. She was convicted of _____ for lying in court.
    A. perjury
    B. strife
    C. ovation
    D. vicissitude

78. Inventing the new machine involved a(n) _____ amount of research and development.
    A. assiduous
    B. indigent
    C. duplicitous
    D. immense

79. The police _____ the door to the apartment so that the search could be carried out.
    A. appeased
    B. covered up
    C. dug up
    D. broke down

80. She is quite _____ at using the computer.
    A. coy
    B. blurry
    C. deft
    D. cogent

81. She had the very strange idea, the _____ that she would win the lottery.
    A. predicament
    B. notion
    C. ambiance
    D. specimen

82. He has had to _____ with many problems in his life.
    A. contend
    B. fidget
    C. procure
    D. flourish

83. The department store was _____ with customers when it reduced its prices by 50%.
    A. inundated
    B. profligate
    C. hushed
    D. abashed

84. What you said really _____ me. Please tell me more.
    A. relegates
    B. intrigues
    C. lingers
    D. subjugates

85. Paula has a(n) _____ for collecting antiques.
    A. insinuation
    B. snag
    C. penchant
    D. dissension

86. Can you read this _____ note?
    A. avid
    B. stagnant
    C. convivial
    D. scribbled

87. The management's decision will certainly have _____ for the employees.
    A. lassitude
    B. plots
    C. overtones
    D. brims

88. She was _____ from singing too much yesterday.
    A. hoarse
    B. pugnacious
    C. neutral
    D. dubious

89. Those who live in poverty experience many hardships and _____.
    A. partitions
    B. lyrics
    C. retreats
    D. setbacks

90. The soldier displayed great _____ in combat.
    A. surplus
    B. dissolution
    C. mettle
    D. diversion

91. He is suffering from a _____ disease.
    A. indignant
    B. parsimonious
    C. contagious
    D. federal

92. Don't _____. Everything will be alright.
    A. smear
    B. fret
    C. scald
    D. fade

93. The _____ was wrapped tightly around the boy's injured hand.
    A. blister
    B. bruise
    C. bandage
    D. bump

94. Use this _____ tape to seal the package.
    A. acute
    B. adhesive
    C. abdominal
    D. ailing

95. He had a deep _____ on his leg which was bleeding profusely.
    A. propensity
    B. spine
    C. gash
    D. cavity

96. Prices _____ during times of scarcity.
    A. recuperate
    B. skyrocket
    C. scorch
    D. splinter

97. John is an incredibly strong and _____ man.
    A. virile
    B. subordinate
    C. ointment
    D. scarlet

98. The situation is _____ , and there is little hope for improvement.
    A. foremost
    B. dispensable
    C. bleak
    D. comprehensive

99. Jane suffered a _____ leg and many other broken bones as a result of the accident.
    A. fractured
    B. shrill
    C. limped
    D. callus

100. His aunt is a very _____ woman and has many unusual habits.
    A. infirm
    B. insurmountable
    C. appliance
    D. unconventional

READING

This passage is about socio-economic status.

Socio-economic status, rather than intellectual ability, may be the key to a child's success later in life, according to a study by Carnegie. Let us consider two hypothetical elementary school students named John and Paul. Both of these children work hard, pay attention in the classroom, and are respectful to their teachers. However, Paul's father is a prosperous business tycoon, while John's has a menial job working in a factory. Solely owing to their disparate economic backgrounds, Paul is nearly 30 times more likely than John to land a high-flying job by the time he reaches his fortieth year, despite the similarities in their academic aptitudes. In fact, John has only a 12% chance of finding and maintaining a job that would earn him even a median-level income.

Research dealing with the economics of inequality among adults supports these findings. These studies also reveal that the economics of inequality is a trend that has become more and more pronounced in recent years. In the mid-twentieth century, the mean after-tax pay for a corporate executive was more than 12 times that of the average factory worker. Today, this situation has reached a level which some economists refer to as "**hyper-inequality**." That is, it is now common for the salary of the average CEO to be more than 100 times that of the typical blue-collar employee.

Because of this and other economic dichotomies, a theoretical stance has recently sprung into existence, asserting that inequality is institutionalized. In keeping with this concept, some researchers argue that workers from higher socio-economic backgrounds are disproportionately compensated, even though the contribution they make to society is no more valuable than *that of their lower-paid counterparts*. To rectify the present imbalance caused by this economic stratification, researchers claim that economic rewards should be judged by and distributed according to the worthiness of the employment to society as a whole. Economic rewards under this framework refer not only to wages or salaries, but also to power, status, and prestige within one's community, as well as within larger society.

Cultural and critical theorists have also joined in the economic debate that empirical researchers embarked upon decades ago. Focusing on the effect of cultural technologies and systems, they state that various forms of media promote the mechanisms of economic manipulation and oppression. Watching television, they claim, causes those of lower socio-economic class to view themselves as apolitical and powerless victims of the capitalistic machine, and thereby has a deleterious impact upon individual identity and human motivation.

101. Which of the following best expresses the main idea of the passage?
    A. Socio-economic status has wide-ranging effects on life and lifestyle, as well as on a number of personal preferences and behaviors.
    B. Socio-economic level primarily affects communication skills.
    C. Socio-economic unfairness results predominantly in lethargy among those most profoundly affected by it.
    D. Socio-economic inequality usually results in premature death to those who experience it.

102. Why does the author mention John and Paul in paragraph 1 of the passage?
    A. to emphasize the needs of blue-collar employees
    B. to illustrate the economic effects of social inequality
    C. to describe how poverty has impacted upon the life of one particular child
    D. to explicate hyper-inequality

103. Based on the information in paragraph 2, which of the following best explains the term "hyper-inequality"?
    A. The fact that the disparity between high and low-level salaries has become so enormous.
    B. The fact that low-level salaries have become bifurcated.
    C. The fact that economists are keenly interested in the subject of financial inequality.
    D. The fact that CEOs have more prestige than factory workers.

104. The words "that of their lower paid counterparts" in paragraph 3 of the passage refer to which of the following?
    A. the inequality which lower-paid workers encounter
    B. the compensation paid to people of lower-level incomes
    C. the salaries of people from affluent socio-economic strata
    D. the benefit to society from the work of lower compensated people

105. Which of the following best expresses the main idea of paragraph 4?
    A. Cultural theorists have expanded upon the work of previous research.
    B. Television and other media have a positive effect on social equality.
    C. Television viewing can reinforce feelings of socio-economic subjugation.
    D. Economic stratification creates social imbalance.

This passage is about acid rain.

Acid has been present in rain for millennia, naturally occurring from volcanoes and plankton. However, scientific research shows that the acid content of rain has increased dramatically over the past two hundred years, in spite of humanity's recent attempts to control the problem.

Rain consists of two elements, nitrogen and sulfur. When sulfur is burned, it transforms into sulfur dioxide. Subsequently, both sulfur dioxide and nitrogen oxide react with the water molecules in rain to form sulfuric acid and nitric acid, respectively. The principal cause of acid rain is sulfur and nitrogen compounds from human sources, like the generation of electricity and emissions from motor vehicles and factories. Industries that utilize coal as a fuel are also among the greatest contributors to the pollutants that cause acid rain. That is to say, the acid in rain emanates from automobile exhaust, domestic residences, and power stations. **The latter have been the culprit of the bulk** of the acid in rainwater in recent years.

Since the pollutants are carried by the wind, countries are now experiencing acid rain from pollution that was generated in countries thousands of miles away. Factories and other enterprises have built high chimneys in an attempt to carry pollutants away from urban areas. Nevertheless, the effect of the structures has been to spread the toxins more thinly and widely in the atmosphere, thereby exacerbating the problem.

Acid rain has inimical impacts on forests, as well as on natural and aquatic life-forms. Research demonstrates that the concentrations of chemicals in acid rain cause damage to fish and other aquatic animals, and biodiversity is reduced as bodies of water become more acidic. Acid rain has even destroyed some insect and fish species in certain areas.

Plants can also be damaged by acid rain, but the effect on crops is ameliorated by regular cultivation and by the application of fertilizers. Forests in high-altitude areas are especially vulnerable as they are often covered by clouds and fog which are more acidic than the rain itself.

106. Which one of the following statements best expresses the main idea of the passage?
   A. Scientific research shows that the acid content of rain has increased dramatically over the past two hundred years.
   B. The principal cause of acid rain is sulfur and nitrogen compounds from human sources.
   C. Forests in high-altitude areas are especially vulnerable as they are often covered by clouds and fog which are more acidic than the rain itself.
   D. This research has been largely pointless since it has done very little to rectify the problem or to reverse the damage that has already been done.

107. What is the major contributor to the problem of acid rain?
   A. ocean life, such as volcanoes and plankton
   B. human activities, such as fuel generation and pollution from homes, vehicles, and factories
   C. the construction of high chimneys
   D. cultivation of plants and application of fertilizers

108. Which one of the following phrases is closest in meaning to the phrase "the latter have been the culprit of the bulk" as it is used in the above passage?
    A. Automobile exhaust, domestic residences, and power stations have equally contributed to the creation of acid rain.
    B. Power stations are more widespread geographically than other causes of acid rain.
    C. Power stations generate a great deal of pollution that is carried by the wind.
    D. Power stations have been the largest contributor to the problem.

109. In what way does acid rain harm fish and ocean life?
    A. It increases the levels of sulfur and nitrogen in the air.
    B. It raises the amount of acid in oceans and other bodies of water.
    C. It spreads polluting gases more thinly and widely.
    D. It has a negative effect on the vegetation that fish use for food.

110. Why does the author mention chimneys in paragraph 3?
    A. to give a scientific explanation for a current problem
    B. to give a chemical analysis of the components of pollution
    C. to talk about an attempted but unsuccessful solution
    D. to show how pollution has increased in urban areas

This passage is about sports.

In my opinion, sports have long been a favorite pastime, if not a fanatical obsession, for people from all walks of life. Not only do sports exist as a source of entertainment for the public, but also as a lucrative business enterprise for those who provide financial backing.

Let me give you one example. Major League Baseball consisted of only a handful of teams when the National League was founded in 1876. It has grown in popularity by leaps and bounds over the years, resulting in increased ticket sales for games and bolstering the profits of its investors. The increased demand from the public, in turn, precipitated the formation of a new division, known as the American League, in 1901.

I should also say that new teams have been formed from time to time in accordance with regional demand; such was the case with the Colorado Rockies in Denver, Colorado, and the Rays in Tampa Bay, Florida.

However, I think we can all agree that the sport which has reaped the largest monetary investment has been American basketball. Successful marketing, together with the aggressive recruitment of new players, helped to enthrall Americans with this sport. With hindsight, it appears that the National Basketball Association (NBA) received the most substantial boost commercially when several new teams were set up. Previously existing teams, such as the Chicago Bulls, also experienced an increase in popularity during that era.

111. According to the passage, which statement best explains why sports have become so popular?
   A. Sports exist solely due to the demand for entertainment displayed by the public.
   B. Sports have become popular only because of monetary assistance provided by various companies.
   C. Sports are profitable for the public.
   D. Sports are enjoyable for people from various strata of society.

112. What is mentioned about American baseball?
    A. It was doomed from the beginning.
    B. It was the result of successful marketing.
    C. It has experienced rapid periodic growth.
    D. It was due to the establishment of new teams.

113. Why have new baseball teams been established from time to time?
    A. because of regulations of the league
    B. as a result of increased ticket sales
    C. due to a reduction in financial support from investors
    D. since there was an increase in the interest of a particular geographical area

114. Which factor contributed to the increased popularity of basketball?
    A. new investors
    B. lackluster marketing
    C. retaining the same players
    D. the historical importance of the sport

115. Which of the following statements accurately describes a specific aspect about sports?
    A. Most people have a sport that they like best.
    B. By examining the past, we can see that the formation of new teams made basketball successful.
    C. The American and National Leagues were formed due to a slump in regional markets.
    D. A higher volume of ticket sales depends upon larger investor expenditures.

This passage is about farming.

Diversification is the key to success in today's agrarian pursuits. Traditionally, farmers have raised livestock such as dairy cows and flocks of sheep, allowing these herbivorous animals to graze in pastures as their primary source of feeding. Today, farmers have augmented their lines of business with a wide range of plants and niche-market animals, and their production methods are often monitored by sophisticated computer programs.

Pedigree dogs are one example of niche-market animals. These animals are normally kept inside kennels, which are usually located in barns or sheds on the premises. Since the dogs are sometimes kept in rather confined quarters, it is imperative to be observant of changes in their temperament. An upset canine may need to be calmed by the human touch or by offering a special treat.

Increasing numbers of fish hatcheries have also sprung into existence in order to fuel our increasing demand for alternative sources of consumable protein. The development of fish is a highly delicate process and must be monitored carefully. The scales of the fish must be examined to ensure that they are of the correct color and consistency. The gills must also be inspected to see that the fish can breathe correctly. Additionally, the fins must be checked to determine whether the fish is able to swim freely.

Other farmers have expanded into the area of horticulture. Specialized lines of production include fruit trees, which are raised in orchards or groves on the farmer's property. These trees are deciduous and lose their leaves every fall. Evergreen trees, on the other hand, are non-deciduous and remain green year-round. Trees such as the spruce, cedar, and pine have become popular for decorative purposes during the December holiday season, making this month an especially hectic time of year for farmers in this business.

Farmers may also wish to use their orchard or grove as a place to keep bees. Beekeeping does have its drawbacks, however, such as the danger of getting stung by the more aggressive inhabitants of the hive.

Whatever line of production is established, cleanliness remains of the utmost importance as no operation will thrive in squalor. All areas must be kept free of the infestation of rodents, especially rats and mice, which may harm both trees and livestock. Finally, methods must be employed for the removal of animal waste.

116. What is the main idea of this passage?
    A. In the past, farmers used to raise cattle for the production of beef.
    B. Farmers need to find a niche market in order to be successful.
    C. Dogs, fish, and fruit are the most profitable market sectors.
    D. In today's agricultural market, farmers usually produce and sell various products.

117. What is mentioned about pedigree dogs?
    A. They may be kept in places that somewhat restrict their movements.
    B. They are not carnivorous in nature.
    C. They are unlikely ever to show signs of aggression.
    D. They are never in need of human contact.

118. Why should fish be examined and checked?
    A. to see if they can inhale and exhale properly through their gills
    B. to check that their scales are fit for the purpose of respiration
    C. to evaluate whether their fins are the proper shade and texture
    D. to ensure that they are easy to sell

119. Which of the following is an aspect of the area of horticulture?
    A. the production of deciduous trees for the holiday season
    B. the harvest of fruit from non-deciduous trees
    C. trees grown in both orchards and groves
    D. the procurement of honey from beehives

120. The problem of hygiene in agricultural environments:
    A. may be rectified by the removal of animal carcasses.
    B. encompasses the dilemma of manure disposal.
    C. results in a squalid atmosphere.
    D. is solved when all pests have been exterminated through the process of fumigation.

ECPE PRACTICE TEST 3

GRAMMAR

1. Once he _____ that he wasn't going to get his old job back, he felt a lot better.
   A. accepts
   B. did accept
   C. will accept
   D. had accepted

2. It would be hard to part _____ your pet.
   A. from
   B. to
   C. with
   D. on

3. - He was really upset about not receiving an invitation.
   - Oh, no! We _____ have invited him!
   A. must
   B. may
   C. should
   D. ought

4. Although some people can't stand her, I can put _____ her sometimes.
   A. down
   B. in for
   C. up with
   D. off

5. I didn't get a raise or a bonus, and _____ .
   A. he didn't though
   B. he did too
   C. neither did he
   D. he did either

6. How about _____ bowling tonight?
   A. to go
   B. we go
   C. going for
   D. going

7. Even though you feel like giving up, you shouldn't throw _____ the towel yet.
   A. out
   B. in
   C. up
   D. down

8. Your socks are in the suitcase _____ you put your shoes.
   A. that
   B. in which
   C. in where
   D. in that

9. This is a clean-air workspace, so smoking is frowned _____ .
   A. down
   B. at
   C. on
   D. against

10. _____ so much, you wouldn't have gotten a stomach ache.
    A. Would you have eaten
    B. Had you not eaten
    C. Should you have eaten
    D. You had not eaten

11. She still hasn't apologized, but she _____ do so soon.
    A. had better
    B. better had to
    C. would rather
    D. should rather

12. I'm afraid her story just _____ hold water.
    A. will hold
    B. doesn't hold
    C. held
    D. is holding

13. _____ painting, she can also draw.
    A. apart
    B. instead
    C. except
    D. besides

14. _____ , he lost his job because the company was having financial problems.
    A. Often happens
    B. As often happens
    C. It often happens
    D. So often happens

15. He hit the nail on the head because his remarks were so _____ .
    A. aptly
    B. to be apt
    C. apt
    D. being apt

16. Trying to find your lost earring on the beach would be _____ a needle in a haystack.
    A. like looking for
    B. like looking at
    C. looking for
    D. looking at

17. The management is tired of employees _____ about all the work they have to do.
    A. to complain
    B. complaints
    C. to have complained
    D. complaining

18. She wouldn't tell me what the problem was, but just kept on beating _____ the bush.
    A. around
    B. inside
    C. at
    D. under

19. - I could go for a pizza tonight
    - Yeah, I _____ one too.
    A. like to have
    B. feel like to have
    C. feel like having
    D. feel like I had

20. I heard that the new health club _____ next week.
    A. be opening
    B. is being opening
    C. will opening
    D. is having its opening

21. She told me about the surprise birthday party, although she _____ .
    A. mightn't have
    B. won't have
    C. ought not to have
    D. couldn't have

22. She has told those lies and many _____ .
    A. other
    B. another
    C. others
    D. anothers

23. He is a funny comedian and _____ many famous celebrities really well.
    A. is imitating
    B. had imitated
    C. imitates
    D. does imitation

24. I didn't get the job since I didn't have _____ required for the job.
    A. most of the skills
    B. most of skills
    C. the most skills
    D. the most of skills

25. I have seen one of Grant Wood's paintings, but I _____ .
    A. from where can't remember
    B. where can't remember
    C. can't remember from where
    D. can't remember where

26. I heard that the party this weekend is going to be _____ a feast.
    A. nothing other than
    B. none else but
    C. nothing than
    D. never other than

27. I couldn't help overhearing him because he has _____ voice.
    A. such a loud
    B. such loud
    C. a such loud
    D. so loud

28. I'm glad you _____ me the bad news, even though it was sad to hear it.
    A. had told
    B. told
    C. were telling
    D. tell

29. - I had a hard day at work.
    - Well, _____ reason to take it out on me!
    A. that's no
    B. this is no
    C. it's for no
    D. for no

30. That talk was far too advanced _____ as an introductory lecture.
    A. to be suiting
    B. for suiting
    C. to be suitable
    D. suitably

31. I'll _____ you at the entrance to the movie theater.
    A. waiting
    B. be waiting for
    C. be waiting
    D. waiting for

32. I know she is still angry with me, but I said I was sorry. What else _____ ?
    A. can be done
    B. I can do
    C. can it be done
    D. can I to do

33. He finally managed to finish college, even though he _____ .
    A. just only passed
    B. just only passed it
    C. only just passed
    D. only just passed that

34. Could you please _____ favorite plaid coat from home?
    A. bring me
    B. bring me my
    C. to bring me my
    D. bring to me

35. He has a very demanding job, so _____ go on vacation.
    A. rarely he goes
    B. goes he rarely
    C. rarely does he go
    D. does rarely he go

36. Next time we'll have to _____ write her name more clearly.
    A. made her
    B. made her to
    C. make her
    D. make her to

37. He's been making a lot of trouble _____ me because we fell out last week.
    A. to
    B. for
    C. against
    D. by

38. I really don't like working with the public, so I was hoping _____ take up a career in the service industry.
    A. I should not
    B. not to have to
    C. not having to
    D. not having

39. - Did Ann lose her job?
    - Yes, and _____ , she is very upset about it.
    A. need less to say
    B. needless to say
    C. less is needed to say
    D. needless by saying

40. He doesn't think it's going to rain today, and _____ .
    A. I don't neither
    B. neither do I
    C. I do either
    D. either don't I

CLOZE

This passage is about actors.

Whether you watch them at home or go out to the movie theater, there are many types of movies to choose from these days. Dramatic films usually (41) well-known stars to attract loyal (42). The leading male and female roles for these movies require high-profile individuals. Therefore, only eminent actors are sought (43) for these roles. Documentaries provide both entertainment and (44) for audiences who want to pass the time pleasantly and learn something new at the same time. Well-spoken male or female professionals work well in (45) roles. Certain productions deal (46) crisis situations, so documentary broadcasters need steady and clear (47) voices in order to provide the commentary for these films. Action and adventure movies are usually good money-makers at the box office. These movies require many actors for (48) roles. "Extras" are also needed for crowd (49) and rehearsals. Work assignments may (50) daily.

41.	a. make	b. feature	c. support	d. claim
42.	a. goers	b. watchers	c. viewers	d. spectators
43.	a. on	b. after	c. with	d. among
44.	a. alienation	b. education	c. tuition	d. pedagogy
45.	a. any	b. fewer	c. work	d. these
46.	a. together	b. with	c. across	d. about
47.	a. speakable	b. spoken	c. speech	d. speaking
48.	a. supportive	b. personable	c. supporting	d. supportable
49.	a. scenes	b. schemes	c. scenery	d. scheming
50.	a. waver	b. wary	c. vacillate	d. vary

This passage is about a recipe.

Today, I would like to share my most-loved recipe: New York Strips. You can make this scrumptious dish (51) home. Simply (52) the steps reproduced in this article. Remember, though, that the instructions must be carried out in the (53) sequence as results cannot be guaranteed if any variations are made. You may wish to (54) down these notes for future reference. The first step is to purchase grade-A steaks. It is of vital importance (55) the meat be fresh. Steer clear of any (56) which have a pale color or are not uniform in size and shape. In addition, dense steaks are preferable to light ones as they generally have a (57) flavor. The steaks must be trimmed (58) fat before broiling. You may wish to sharpen a knife beforehand for this purpose. Once trimmed, the steaks should be browned under a broiler (59) they are medium to well done. Remember to place a receptacle underneath to catch the grease. Herbs and seasonings, like fresh basil, oregano, and garlic, can be (60) if you choose to brown your steak in a skillet.

51. a. at   b. to   c. in   d. within
52. a. bring   b. keep   c. follow   d. join
53. a. extract   b. exact   c. exacting   d. retract
54. a. clip   b. jot   c. dot   d. blot
55. a. that   b. as   c. for   d. which
56. a. slashes   b. clips   c. slits   d. cuts
57. a. whole   b. fuller   c. entire   d. fullest
58. a. of   b. with   c. by   d. to
59. a. since   b. until   c. yet   d. during
60. a. maintained b. neglected   c. included   d. manufactured

VOCABULARY

61. This club accepts members from all _____ of life.
    A. leaps
    B. walks
    C. strides
    D. jumps

62. The economy has recently been _____ by an increase in tourism.
    A. flopped
    B. reaped
    C. bolstered
    D. ventured

63. With _____, I can see now that I shouldn't have gone to the party last night.
    A. retrospect
    B. viewing
    C. vision
    D. hindsight

64. His father's death _____ his decision to manage the family business.
    A. precipitated
    B. vied
    C. enthralled
    D. recruited

65. When his second novel was published, he felt that he had really made the _____ time.
    A. big
    B. huge
    C. lucrative
    D. boom

66. She has proved to be a _____-weather friend. She didn't help me at the time I needed it most.
    A. hard
    B. foul
    C. fair
    D. poor

67. The country's _____ policy is established by the director of banking at the Federal Reserve Board.
    A. contingent
    B. memorabilia
    C. arduous
    D. monetary

68. The store specializes in formal _____ for men and women, including suits and dresses.
    A. apparel
    B. whims
    C. fads
    D. enterprises

69. The number of women in the work force has grown by _____ and bounds in recent years.
    A. jumps
    B. leaps
    C. walks
    D. steps

70. He is a _____ fan of his local football team. He never misses a game.
    A. fickle
    B. hard-core
    C. defunct
    D. hard

71. Ellen is so _____ in the morning that you should never attempt to speak to her until the afternoon.
    A. temperamental
    B. trend
    C. commercial
    D. hamlet

72. The current _____ in fashion indicates that bright colors will be in style this year.
    A. potential
    B. trend
    C. vindication
    D. hamlet

73. Thanks to the _____ of fire departments from the surrounding cities, the blaze was stopped in time.
    A. proliferation
    B. conjugation
    C. evaluation
    D. collaboration

74. There is always a(n) _____ of food at Thanksgiving Day celebrations.
    A. entity
    B. subscription
    C. overabundance
    D. fluctuation

75. Judging from the way she _____ her pancakes, I'd say that she hadn't eaten in three days.
    A. devoured
    B. spawned
    C. thwarted
    D. surged

76. She was completely _____ in the television program she was watching.
    A. undaunted
    B. absorbed
    C. sticky
    D. accosted

77. Anyone wishing to work for the government must first undergo a(n) _____ background investigation.
    A. tiny
    B. stringent
    C. handy
    D. stingy

78. If you approach the job with_____, you should be able to finish it more quickly.
    A. alacrity
    B. vulgarity
    C. reluctance
    D. wholesomeness

79. The media's emphasis on health and fitness has caused many new gyms to spring _____ .
    A. out
    B. up
    C. around
    D. forward

80. Florence Nightingale's devotion to the sick was _____.
    A. waved
    B. wavering
    C. waving
    D. unwavering

81. She was a _____ artist and created many paintings throughout her lifetime.
    A. subsequent
    B. prodigious
    C. tardy
    D. reticent

82. He is such a lazy person that he doesn't have the _____ to accomplish anything.
    A. drive
    B. enrollment
    C. congruity
    D. prerogative

83. What a(n) _____ idea! I wish I'd thought of it.
    A. cumbersome
    B. mandatory
    C. provincial
    D. ingenious

84. The ceremony _____ at 9:00 and lasts until 11:00.
    A. compels
    B. prompts
    C. commences
    D. fetters

85. The main _____ of the plan is its high expense.
    A. drawback
    B. conjugation
    C. providence
    D. vocation

86. Her _____ is to become a famous classical pianist.
    A. hindrance
    B. solicitation
    C. accommodation
    D. aspiration

87. The president gave the _____ for the enactment of the new law.
    A. sponsor
    B. size up
    C. contemporary
    D. go-ahead

88. They _____ the child to go to the party by promising him candy.
    A. expelled
    B. enticed
    C. partook
    D. widespread

89. The _____ total of the company's yearly profit is $850,000.
    A. cumulative
    B. flexible
    C. accessible
    D. widespread

90. Her job is very demanding and extremely _____.
    A. trying
    B. registration
    C. accumulated
    D. provident

91. The two enemies had been _____ for years.
    A. ensigns
    B. adversaries
    C. advocates
    D. inhabitants

92. John was _____ when his job application was rejected.
    A. demoralized
    B. lauded
    C. invigorated
    D. flanked

93. Teachers are advised to avoid _____ topics, such as politics and religion, in classroom discussions.
    A. intrepid
    B. affiliation
    C. controversial
    D. innocuous

94. The teams from the two state universities had engaged in friendly _____ for years.
   A. treason
   B. pillage
   C. frontiers
   D. rivalry

95. Drug addiction ultimately led to his _____.
   A. downfall
   B. armistice
   C. proposition
   D. patriotism

96. Where did you come up with such a crazy _____?
   A. blunder
   B. draft
   C. notion
   D. civilian

97. The actor was dressed in formal _____ for the charity event.
   A. era
   B. skirmish
   C. attire
   D. corpse

98. The _____ was standing guard at the front gate.
   A. secession
   B. sentry
   C. combat
   D. reconnaissance

99. It is _____ that you are lying. Why don't you tell the truth?
    A. apparent
    B. consolidated
    C. domesticated
    D. divergent

100. Animals such as lions and tigers are _____ .
    A. perpetrators
    B. lackadaisical
    C. infantile
    D. predators

READING

This passage is about social trends.

Recent research has revealed some significant social trends relating to immigration and population. Notably, the population tripled from almost 76 million at the beginning of the twentieth century to nearly 281 million at the start of the twenty-first century. Average household size declined by 2 people per household over the last century, from 4.6 people per household a hundred years ago to 2.6 members per household today.

Population density has increased two-fold during the last one hundred years, but remains relatively low in comparison to most other countries in the world. Alaska had the lowest population density, and the population density of the Northeast, which has always been high, continued consistently to outstrip that of other regional areas. While most of the population lived outside cities prior to the end of World War II, the percentage of the population living in metropolitan areas increased in every subsequent decade of the study. New York and California had the largest populations, and Florida and Arizona had the fastest-growing populations during the period of the study.

Previously, the majority of households were living in the Northeast and Midwest, but since 1980 the majority was in the South and West. Slightly more than half of all households are now maintained by people aged 45 and over. Female householders have increased as a proportion of all householders, and older females were far more likely to live alone than were men or younger women. The per capita marriage rate has fallen in the last fifteen years, and there was a concurrent drop in the per capita divorce rate during this time.

The survey also examined changes to overall national income, as well as the spending habits of individuals and households. It has found that the distribution of income has become more and more unequal over the past forty years, with the income of the richest 10% of the people in the country rising disproportionately to that of the poorest sector of the population. As relatively worse-off households struggle to make essential purchases, the amount of consumer credit has recently increased to over a trillion dollars, with credit cards and revolving credit arrangements constituting the lion's share of this figure. Cash transactions fell sharply as innovative technologies and new forms of payment appeared in the marketplace.

101. According to passage, what was the most dramatic change to the population in the last one hundred years?
    A. The three-fold increase in the size of the population
    B. The increase in average household size
    C. The worryingly high rise in population density
    D. The low population density in Alaska

102. Why does the author mention the changes to the populations of Florida and Arizona?
    A. to point out that new residents are continually moving to these states
    B. to contrast their population changes to those in New York and California
    C. to exemplify the increase in the percentage of the population living in metropolitan areas
    D. to illustrate why people wish to leave the Northeast and Midwest

103. What is the most likely interpretation of the cause of changes to the marriage and divorce rates?
    A. The marriage rate went down because more women preferred to live alone.
    B. The divorce rate went down because fewer people got married during the period of the study.
    C. The marriage rate went down because the core of the population is aging.
    D. The divorce rate declined because existing marriages became more stable.

104. According to passage, which is the most significant demographic change when comparing geographic areas?
    A. Female householders rose as a percentage of all householders.
    B. Older females live alone more often than do men or younger women.
    C. Many people moved from the Northeast and Midwest to live in the South or West.
    D. The population declined sharply in California and New York over the course of the study.

105. According to the passage, what could be inferred about why more older women live alone?
    A. Women are preoccupied about the needs of their children, so they deprioritize other relationships.
    B. Women generally suffer from a decline in household income after the breakup of a relationship.
    C. Women are more likely to live alone after losing a long-term life partner than men are.
    D. The social stigma of divorce is greater for women than men.

This passage is about the electron microscope.

An efficient electron microscope can magnify an object by more than one million times its original size. This innovation has thereby allowed scientists to study the precise molecules that constitute human life.

The electron microscope functions by emitting a stream of electrons from a gun-type instrument which is similar to the apparatus used in an old-fashioned television tube. The electrons pass through an advanced electronic field that is accelerated to millions of volts in certain cases. Before traveling through a vacuum in order to remove oxygen molecules, the electrons are focused into a beam by way of magnetic coils.

Invisible to the naked eye, electron beams can be projected onto a florescent screen. When striking the screen, the electrons glow and can even be recorded on film. Analog cameras also use film to capture images.

In the transmission electron microscope, which is used to study cells or tissues, the beam passes through a thin slice of the specimen that is being studied. On the other hand, in the scanning electron microscope, which is used for tasks such as examining bullets and fibers, the beam is reflected. This reflection creates a picture of the specimen line by line.

106. What is this passage mainly about?
    A. the function of different kinds of electron microscopes
    B. the history of all of the various types of microscopes
    C. the reason why the electron microscope was invented
    D. the movement of electrons and electronic beams

107. What is the last step in the process by which the beam emanating from the electron microscope is formed?
    A. the electrons pass through a television tube.
    B. the electrons are accelerated to millions of volts.
    C. the electrons travel through a vacuum.
    D. the electrons pass through magnetic coils.

108. What is mentioned about electronic beams?
    A. They are used in some types of guns.
    B. They cannot be seen without special equipment.
    C. They are used in cameras.
    D. They are more important in the transmission electron microscope.

109. What does the author think about the electron microscope?
    A. The electron microscope has proven to be an extremely important invention for the scientific community.
    B. The invention of the electron microscope would have been impossible without the prior invention of the television.
    C. The electron microscope cannot function without projection onto a florescent screen.
    D. The transmission electron microscope is inferior to the scanning electron microscope.

110. What best describes the purpose of the final paragraph of the passage?
    A. to compare the transmission and electron microscopes
    B. to show that specimens need to be thin in order to be examined
    C. to explain that electrons can be reflected
    D. to emphasize the importance of examining bullets and fibers

This passage is about the court system.

Many steps are required in successfully prosecuting a criminal case in the present legal system. Once the crime has been committed and discovered, the police force is dispatched to the crime scene to begin the investigation. Simultaneously, any possible suspects or witnesses are taken in for questioning at the local police precinct having jurisdiction over the case.

Suspects and witnesses can be subjected to mild inquisition or full-scale interrogation, depending upon the severity of the matter. During this time, suspects might be held in detention until their denial of the crime, or alibi, can be verified. In the event that a confession is given or enough evidence is uncovered to incriminate the suspect, he or she will be charged with the crime, if there are no extenuating circumstances. Thereafter, the suspect is taken into custody or released on bail.

The case is then prosecuted in court. Many witnesses testify during the trial, giving testimony to implicate or exonerate the accused. When the judge strikes his or her gavel, he or she thereby indicates that the jury should recess for impartial deliberation of the verdict.

The jury may find the accused innocent of the crime, whereupon he or she will be acquitted and released. On the other hand, ***they*** might find the accused guilty of the crime. If so, the accused is then formally convicted of the crime, sentenced to the appropriate number of years for the violation, and imprisoned.

111. What is an aspect of the present legal system?
    A. A criminal case begins when the suspect is sued.
    B. The legal process consists of various systematic phases.
    C. The case is prosecuted at the local police precinct.
    D. It is only utilized for the most serious crimes.

112. Which one of the following conclusions can be made from the passage?
    A. Suspects and witnesses may receive different degrees of questioning.
    B. Law enforcement divisions from various neighborhoods have authority over the case.
    C. Suspects receive more intense questioning than witnesses.
    D. The amount of questioning presented to the suspects and witnesses is standard from case to case.

113. What does the author mention about witnesses?
    A. They have to give a sworn statement in court during the trial.
    B. They are held in custody while their testimony is investigated.
    C. They serve time in detention with suspects.
    D. They are prosecuted in court.

114. What happens after a suspect is charged with a crime?
    A. he or she will be required to do time in jail.
    B. he or she will always be released on bail.
    C. he or she may be taken into custody.
    D. evidence is discovered to implicate him or her.

115. To which of the following does the word *they* in the final paragraph refer?
    A. the accused
    B. the crimes
    C. the jury
    D. the witnesses

This passage is about healthcare.

The question of how to obtain affordable, comprehensive healthcare is foremost in the minds of many people at present. A system of socialized medicine which operates in affiliation with the government is not yet widely available to the public in our country. Therefore, many individuals and families participate in private health insurance plans.

Without adequate insurance coverage, a patient afflicted with a heart ailment, for example, may find it difficult to afford a by-pass or transplant operation. In addition, individuals who suffer from chronic conditions, such as cardiac issues, diabetes, or arthritis, may find the cost of insurance premiums insurmountable, so they may be able to participate in state-sponsored insurance plans. Programs known as high-risk insurance pools and pre-existing condition plans have been established by many states to deal with situations such as these.

The dysfunction of the current system has caused the price of prescription medications to skyrocket to an exorbitant level. Any uninsured individual who requires medicine on a daily basis might even encounter difficulties in finding a pharmacy to dispense the medication.

Perhaps the most unfortunate victims of the current system are the elderly. It is natural for senior citizens to fall prey to various infirmities during old age, but something is seriously amiss when an elderly patient is discharged from the hospital prematurely to recuperate at home because he or she is not adequately insured. Many believe the present system is not beyond reproach. Some have argued that if the healthcare system cannot provide care for those who need it most, namely the feeble and frail, it is of no real use whatsoever.

116. What is the main idea of the passage?
    A. Individuals and families wishing to use the health system will normally need to have adequate insurance.
    B. The health system is funded in alliance with various hospitals.

C. The health system is funded by tax-deductible charitable donations.

D. The health system is under scrutiny by various major insurance companies.

117. Which of the following patients will usually come across difficulties in obtaining treatment?
    A. a person who does not have full insurance coverage
    B. a person participating in a state-sponsored plan
    C. a person participating in a high-risk insurance pool
    D. a person who requires medicine on a daily basis

118. What is mentioned about an individual who suffers from arthritis?
    A. He or she could be required to pay a higher fee for his or her insurance.
    B. He or she may become reliant on the federal government.
    C. He or she will inevitably seek financial assistance from national medical agencies.
    D. He or she will be unable to obtain medication.

119. According to the passage, what can happen to senior citizens?
    A. They usually overstay their welcome at the hospital.
    B. They normally bounce back after receiving treatment.
    C. They are admitted to the hospital too early.
    D. They are sometimes forced to convalesce at home.

120. Which word would best describe the current state of affairs of the health system, according to the author?
    A. subordinate
    B. indignant
    C. amiable
    D. troubled

ECPE PRACTICE TEST 4

GRAMMAR

1. You must refrain _____ smoking in any of the buildings in the hospital complex.
   A. from
   B. for
   C. against
   D. to

2. She passed out from the heat, but they managed to bring her _____.
   A. around
   B. up
   C. down
   D. on

3. I didn't like all of the terms of the contract, so I decided to bail _____ the agreement.
   A. off
   B. out of
   C. through
   D. up against

4. _____ knowledge, you can travel to Chicago on Route 66.
   A. To my best
   B. In the best
   C. In my best
   D. To the best of my

5. He is clearly _____ his three brothers.
   A. more intelligent of
   B. the most intelligent
   C. more intelligent than
   D. the most intelligent of

6. She is self-centered and has no respect for anyone else's feelings _____.
   A. moreover
   B. whatsoever
   C. however
   D. insomuch as

7. I really regret _____ harder to increase my savings when I was younger.
   A. not having tried
   B. not to try
   C. not to tried
   D. not to trying

8. Success usually hinges upon hard work and _____ .
   A. determining
   B. determination
   C. determinations
   D. a determination

9. - Have you noticed that John is getting a bit deaf?
   - Yes, I have. He _____ me to repeat something four times yesterday.
   A. had asked
   B. asked
   C. has been asking
   D. had been asking

10. Your keys are on top of the cupboard _____ we put the dishes.
    A. where
    B. which
    C. that
    D. in that

11. We couldn't have finished the project without him because he _____ a great deal of expertise to the job.
    A. brought
    B. had brought
    C. will have brought
    D. will be bringing

12. Not a word _____ by the employees during the meeting yesterday.
    A. they did speak
    B. was speaking
    C. was spoken
    D. was it spoken

13. I didn't get a good mark on the exam because I needed to have _____ .
    A. prepared thoroughly more
    B. thoroughly more prepared
    C. thorough preparation more
    D. prepared more thoroughly

14. I expect her _____ out of her parent's house now that she has finished college.
    A. to move
    B. moving
    C. being moved
    D. to have been moving

15. I _____ this essay three times, so I am dreading doing it again.
    A. had yet re-written
    B. re-wrote already
    C. have already re-written
    D. re-written already

16. _____ , it rains when we have planned a picnic.
    A. Often or not
    B. As often as not
    C. Often as it is not
    D. As often as ever

17. - Thank goodness your friend gave us a hand.
    - I know. _____ , we never would have managed.
    A. But for her help
    B. However her help
    C. But her having helped
    D. Without helping her

18. He is taking his driving test tomorrow, and _____ him so worried.
    A. never have I seen
    B. never I saw
    C. I have seen never
    D. I saw never

19. Our new business going quite well now that we have acquired all _____ we need to sell.
    A. merchandise
    B. the merchandise
    C. a merchandise
    D. of merchandise

20. I don't know _____ from their house to ours, so I couldn't say when they are going to arrive.
    A. how it is far
    B. it is how far
    C. how far it is
    D. how far is it

21. These caves are believed _____ over a million years ago.
    A. to be formed
    B. to have formed
    C. to have been forming
    D. to have been formed

22. The employment rate in this state is _____ most other states.
    A. as same in
    B. the same as that of
    C. same as that
    D. as same as

23. He gets _____ grades of all the students in his class.
    A. the best
    B. the better
    C. the best of
    D. better than

24. The forecast is for inclement weather tomorrow, and _____ , we will have to call off the field trip.
    A. in case of this
    B. if that is the case
    C. for that case
    D. if it's the case

25. It is clear that _____ maintain high standards for our city, then local taxes must be raised.
    A. because it is important
    B. rather than
    C. if we are to
    D. whether they can

26. Scientists are studying white blood cells, _____ protect against disease.
    A. whose purpose it is to
    B. which purpose is
    C. their purpose is to
    D. which have a purpose in order

27. Those plants are said _____ from Australia.
    A. to having imported
    B. to have been imported
    C. to have imported
    D. to being imported

28. - When is your grandma coming to visit?
    - Hopefully, _____ the beginning of the month.
    A. in
    B. at
    C. inside
    D within

29. I am annoyed with him because he told me off _____ , which he always does himself.
    A. to be late
    B. to being late
    C. for being late
    D. being late

30. We hope to go to Florida next month, and I'm sure that _____ there will be a lot of fun.
    A. to go
    B. going
    C. to be going
    D. having gone

31. _____ that he was hurt and needed help, we would have rushed right over.
    A. Had we known
    B. If we did know
    C. We had to know
    D. We had known

32. I am working on the gardening right now, but the grass _____ yet.
    A. hasn't been mown
    B. hadn't mown
    C. haven't mown
    D. haven't being mown

33. - Have you got enough furniture for your new apartment?
    - No, I need _____ more.
    A. many
    B. much
    C. a few
    D. several

34. The trees are really damaged in this neighborhood because _____ a big storm last night.
    A. it was
    B. it happened
    C. there was
    D. there happened

35. I shouldn't trust him anymore because he didn't pay the money back to me. _____ , I still do.
   A. Nonetheless
   B. Never mind less
   C. Neither the less
   D. Nothing less

36. She is my _____ true friend.
   A. one the only
   B. only one of
   C. one and only
   D. one of only

37. He is quite opinionated and can be a bit bossy, but _____ that I like him.
   A. apart from
   B. except from
   C. besides from
   D. apart for

38. I didn't like the movie due to the fact that the ending just wasn't _____ .
   A. enough surprising
   B. surprisingly
   C. surprising enough
   D. surprised enough

39. _____ anyone noticed that you were absent from class today.
   A. Almost
   B. Hardly
   C. Not did
   D. Barely

40. The flight finally took off, but only after _____ two hours.
    A. being delayed
    B. delaying
    C. it's delay
    D. it's delaying

CLOZE

This passage is about television programs.

The overwhelming (41) in the popularity of television in the has spawned the appearance of a plethora of new television networks in cities all (42) the nation. A new (43) of digital networks first appeared in the (44) 1990's as Americans became increasingly (45) by the box. In contrast to the national networks, digital TV is not offered free of (46) to the public, and each subscriber must pay a monthly fee. A subscriber is (47) a local satellite system or uses a cable connected to his or her TV, which is installed in the home. In certain areas, well (48) 500 channels are available. These include companies such as Netflix and Hulu, for which the subscriber is charged a fee in addition to the basic monthly amount. Movies are also (49) on a "pay-per-view" basis where the subscriber can pay for each movie he or she watches, just as he or she would at the (50) theater.

41.	a. surf	b. turf	c. surge	d. splurge
42.	a. within	b. across	c. inside	d. throughout
43.	a. breed	b. essence	c. condition	d. license
44.	a. ending	b. closing	c. final	d. late
45.	a. marred	b. barred	c. absorbed	d. abhorred
46.	a. payment	b. subscription	c. charge	d. fee
47.	a. linked to	b. fitted with	c. joined	d. hooked
48.	a. beyond	b. surpass	c. over	d. past
49.	a. ready	b. limited	c. necessary	d. available
50.	a. movie	b. show	c. cinema	d. film

This passage is about the US and Vietnam.

The United States' involvement in Vietnam (51) one of the most turbulent (52) controversial eras in American history. Advocates (53) intervention asserted the need to assist those in need in southern Asia. Opponents (54) that the United States should not interfere with or attempt to police the political (55) of other countries around the world. Many proponents predicted (56) the conflict would culminate (57) a speedy resolution. However, it quickly became evident that the (58) war was to become a (59) proposition. Many veterans continue to (60) physiological and psychological problems today as a result of their ordeals.

51. a. represents   b. resembled   c. represented   d. resemblance
52. a. and   b. whereas   c. or   d. although
53. a. to   b. of   c. with   d. about
54. a. exacerbated   b. repeated   c. emphasized   d. reiterated
55. a. affiliations   b. exasperation   c. implications   d. concatenation
56. a. which   b. that   c. for   d. when
57. a. to   b. as   c. in   d. from
58. a. succeeded   b. followed   c. ensuing   d. further
59. a. impacted   b. protracted   c. retracted   d. detracted
60. a. meet   b. face up   c. experience   d. experiment

VOCABUALRY

61. No variations should be made from the written _____.
    A. endowment
    B. script
    C. auspices
    D. adornment

62. The professor _____ on the details of the assignment.
    A. elaborated
    B. disjointed
    C. contrived
    D. procured

63. A lot of cotton is _____ in the southern states, particularly Georgia.
    A. underdeveloped
    B. contravened
    C. refrained
    D. produced

64. He is a(n) _____ authority on the subject of nuclear physics.
    A. eminent
    B. licentious
    C. racy
    D. odious

65. Bob is a(n) _____ person and enjoys meeting new people.
    A. bashful
    B. colossal
    C. affable
    D. momentous

66. The _____ plan contained many details and complications.
    A. fervid
    B. winsome
    C. intricate
    D. demeanor

67. The _____ robbed the bank, killing two people.
    A. commentator
    B. coordinator
    C. rehearsal
    D. villain

68. _____ with others is essential for effective teamwork.
    A. Disposition
    B. Extravagance
    C. Procurement
    D. Cooperation

69. The Ford company was once the _____ in the automotive industry.
    A. materialization
    B. forerunner
    C. nudity
    D. obtainment

70. The vacation in the Bahamas that they had planned failed to _____.
    A. contrive
    B. endow
    C. refrain
    D. materialize

71. She is _____ well in her position with the law firm.
    A. simulated
    B. remunerated
    C. contaminated
    D. fabricated

72. It is difficult to concentrate when you are talking _____ .
    A. latently
    B. perpetually
    C. patently
    D. assembly

73. This machine has a _____ which prevents it from functioning properly.
    A. defect
    B. fume
    C. fabric
    D. chassis

74. The final exam will _____ material from Chapters 1 to 8.
    A. conform
    B. patronize
    C. install
    D. encompass

75. She wore a(n) _____ fur coat to the movie theater.
    A. ostentatious
    B. contemporary
    C. innovative
    D. spacious

76. Our house is _____ enough to accommodate 20 people.
    A. tangible
    B. exclusive
    C. roomy
    D. conspicuous

77. He sat by the seashore, _____ his life.
    A. imposing
    B. contemplating
    C. implementing
    D. flaunting

78. This pipe has been _____ with a special protective coating.
    A. galvanized
    B. dented
    C. rusted
    D. hinged

79. Due to a problem with the oven, the house was filled with a _____ gas.
    A. luxurious
    B. stuffy
    C. sleek
    D. noxious

80. One of his _____ is that he is always pulling on his left ear.
    A. obstacles
    B. consumers
    C. quirks
    D. pittances

81. He is currently being _____ for armed robbery.
    A. dispatched
    B. suspected
    C. prosecuted
    D. subjected

82. Her _____ of the crime was clear and convincing.
    A. dispatch
    B. denial
    C. detention
    D. interrogation

83. The judge lessened the sentence for the crime due to _____ circumstances.
    A. extenuating
    B. incriminating
    C. implicating
    D. swindling

84. The _____ attacked his victim with a knife.
    A. ringleader
    B. testament
    C. counterfeiter
    D. assailant

85. Parking fines are not considered to be serious _____ of the law.
    A. rehabilitations
    B. ordinances
    C. deterrents
    D. infringements

86. The suspect was _____ for the crime and was found innocent.
    A. recessed
    B. exonerated
    C. deliberated
    D. deranged

87. They _____ the baby with kisses.
    A. strangled
    B. paroled
    C. smothered
    D. baffled

88. His dad is one of the most _____ parents I know.
    A. lenient
    B. remorseful
    C. fraudulent
    D. blunt

89. The accused criminal was released on _____ .
    A. custody
    B. testimony
    C. bail
    D. jury

90. That crime occurred in our _____.
    A. witness
    B. precinct
    C. gavel
    D. denomination

91. Volunteers were sent out on a(n) _____ to the famine area in Africa.
   A. refectory
   B. interment
   C. mission
   D. tenet

92. The accident victim was lying _____ by the side of the road.
   A. prostrate
   B. slovenly
   C. abstemiously
   D. astray

93. All members of the armed forces must _____ the laws of the country.
   A. denounce
   B. defile
   C. ransom
   D. affirm

94. The _____ of the new factory will bring new jobs to the community.
   A. platform
   B. advent
   C. penitence
   D. rite

95. A two year _____ comes with my new computer.
   A. guarantee
   B. celibacy
   C. convent
   D. dirge

96. The right-wing group _____ the government currently in power and attempted to overthrow it.
    A. exalted
    B. repented
    C. assuaged
    D. renounced

97. Her father died three years ago. In other words, he has been _____ for three years.
    A. deceased
    B. tenet
    C. asunder
    D. pious

98. Any _____ should possess common knowledge of first aid.
    A. congregation
    B. mortuary
    C. zealot
    D. layperson

99. The _____ came into the auditorium at the start of the ceremony.
    A. procession
    B. extermination
    C. recession
    D. inspiration

100. The _____ doctor allowed the patient to undergo therapy, rather than endure more pain.
    A. omnipotent
    B. merciful
    C. temporal
    D. chaste

READING

This passage is about Marie Curie.

In a run-down laboratory near Paris, Marie Curie worked around the clock to discover a radioactive element. To begin her search, she started by studying chemical compounds that contained uranium. In so doing, Curie found that the strength of the rays that were emitted depended solely on the quantity of uranium in the compound. The strength of the rays had no connection with whether the uranium was solid or liquid, or whether the material was pure or combined with other chemical elements. In other words, she discerned that the intensity of radiation present in uranium derived from the uranium atoms themselves, regardless of how the atoms were treated.

This revelation was very significant because normal chemical properties changed according to how a substance was treated. At that time, scientists were aware that such properties came about because of the way atoms combined with one another. However, most scientists believed that the atoms themselves could not possibly be altered. Pondering this, Curie hypothesized that something was happening inside uranium atoms that gave rise to rays. Trying out various chemicals, Curie found that compounds that contained the element thorium also gave off rays.

On the day that she made her discovery, she was blending chemical compounds that could be used to destroy unhealthy cells in the body. As she was about to retire to bed that evening, she decided to return to her lab. There she found that the chemical compound had become crystalized in the bowls and was emitting the elusive light that she sought. Having finally captured her **quarry** in 1902, she named it "radium" after the Latin word meaning ray. To describe the behavior of this chemical element, Curie coined the term "radioactivity."

Inspired by the French scientist Henri Becquerel, Curie won the Nobel Prize for Chemistry in 1903. Upon winning the prize, she declared that the radioactive element would be used only to treat disease and would not be used for commercial profit. Today radium provides the most effective remedy for certain types of cancer. Radium, now used for a treatment called radiation therapy, works by inundating diseased cells with radioactive particles. Its success lies in the fact that it eradicates malignant cells without any lasting ill effects on the body.

101. Which of the following best explains how normal chemical properties could change according to how a substance was treated?
    A. The behavior of the atoms alone could be changed, although extensive experimentation was necessary.
    B. The strength of radiation present in chemical elements was derived from the atoms themselves.
    C. The behavior of atoms could be changed when two or more chemical compounds were combined.
    D. Uranium gave off rays only when it was chemically manipulated.

102. What can be inferred from the fact that the element thorium also gave off rays?
    A. Curie deduced that the chemical properties of thorium were similar to those of uranium.
    B. Curie was discouraged that it was impossible to isolate the particular atom that emitted radiation.
    C. Curie realized that thorium, like uranium, had to be combined with other elements in order to function correctly.
    D. Curie discovered that thorium and uranium would give off rays only if they were mixed together as a chemical compound and then left to crystallize in bowls.

103. In paragraph 3, to what does the word "quarry" refer?
    A. a precious commodity
    B. an unknown catalyst
    C. an object that is sought
    D. a chemical compound

104. Which of the following explains why radium is the most effective remedy for certain types of cancer?
    A. Radium is cost effective.
    B. Radium destroys cancerous cells.
    C. Radium has no long-term effects.
    D. Radium derives from a radioactive element.

105. What is mentioned about the Nobel Prize?
    A. It was won by Henri Becquerel.
    B. It is awarded solely for treatments that are not used for commercial profit.
    C. It is granted only to those who conduct research into radioactive elements.
    D. It was given to Marie Curie in 1903.

This passage is about the educational system.

Working parents have *prompted* widespread growth in the educational system. It is now common for children from both middle-class and well-to-do families to begin nursery school at the age of two, or even younger. Most parents also seize the opportunity to send their children to pre-school subsequent to nursery school. Neither of these educational programs, which are operated independently by private organizations, are mandatory. In fact, state-sponsored education is not usually compulsory until a child is five years old. At this time, the child is required to attend kindergarten at the public elementary school in the district where his parents reside. The child will normally remain at elementary school until the sixth grade. However, prodigious students may advance more quickly if given the go-ahead by the school principal.

Junior high or middle school, which generally comprises the seventh and eighth grades, commences after the completion of elementary school. During these years, a student is not only compelled to attend normal academic courses, but also has the prerogative to choose from a wide range of extra-curricular activities, such as musical groups and athletic teams.

Non-academic activities remain prevalent throughout high school, although some parents view these activities as a hindrance to the learning process. Indeed, students with aspirations of going to college must size up their academic program quite carefully during this educational period. Most students will solicit the advice of the school's academic guidance counsellor to receive information about the admissions criteria of various colleges, as well as to seek help in registering for their college admissions tests. On the other hand, students without the drive to attend college upon graduation may choose to partake in various vocational courses offered through the local community college.

106. What is mentioned about nursery and pre-school programs?
    A. They are required by the state government.
    B. They are attended by children from various economic levels of society.
    C. They have developed slowly over time.
    D. They have been established by working parents.

107. According to the passage, what is true about elementary school?
    A. Before attending elementary school, a child is required to attend pre-school.
    B. Parents can choose which elementary school their child will attend.
    C. Intellectually gifted students can be promoted if given approval by the principal.
    D. A child can decide which public elementary school to attend.

108. What is mentioned about middle school?
    A. It is necessary for a student to participate in non-academic activities.
    B. Students can be expelled for tardiness.
    C. Students should make a tentative decision about attending college.
    D. Students are required to attend the set curriculum.

109. What happens when students who do not wish to attend college?
    A. They need to consult with the school guidance counsellor.
    B. They are more strongly encouraged to participate in after-school activities.
    C. They can attend classes to obtain work-related training.
    D. They must take a college admissions test.

110. What does the writer's use of the word *prompted* in paragraph 1 suggest?
    A. The practice of state-sponsored education has recently experienced a revival.
    B. The parents are determined to change the system.
    C. The children are brought up by the parents.
    D. The parents have caused the demand for and growth in education.

This passage is about tourism.

Adventurers, fieldworkers, volunteers, and travelers are rapidly replacing tourists. However, the tourist will never completed vanish. While those who quietly travel for nothing other than their own enjoyment will continue to do so, it will be a *clandestine* and frowned upon activity. Soon, no one will want to admit to being one of those people.

The World Tourism Organization (WTO) has predicted that by the year 2050, there will be 1.56 billion tourists per year traveling somewhere in the world. This forecast demonstrates the immense challenge in trying to curb the global demand for tourism. In fact, the task may be so tremendous that it might just be impossible.

Some argue that the government should intervene, but the government alone would face huge impediments in attempting to make so many economically-empowered people stop doing something they enjoy. Others assert that tourism is of such extreme damage to the welfare of the world that only totally irresponsible individuals would even consider doing it. Yet, this argument is clearly absurd. Whatever benefits or otherwise accrue from tourism, it is not evil, despite what a tiny minority might say. It can cause harm. It can be neutral, and it can occasionally bring about something good.

Because of these debates, tourism is under attack by more a more oblique method: it has been re-named. Bit by bit, the word "tourist" is being removed from the tourism industry. Since tourism has changed, so too must the vacation. Adventurers, fieldwork assistants, and volunteers do not go on vacations. These new travelers go on "cultural experiences", "expeditions," or "projects". However, re-branding tourism in this way gives freedom to travelers, as well as restrictions.

New travelers express great interest in respecting the environments they visit. They avoid tourist infrastructures because they are afraid of being viewed negatively by the local culture. Instead, they prefer accommodation arrangements such as cabins or camping. These types of accommodation, they believe, are more respectful of local culture. Local culture is very important to the new tourist, whereas the mass tourist is believed to destroy it.

Nevertheless, all types of tourism should be responsible towards and respectful of environmental and human resources. Some tourism developers, as well as individual tourists, have not acted with this in mind. Consequently, a divide is being driven between those few affluent and privileged tourists and the remaining majority.

111. What is this passage mainly about?
    A. Tourism and the environment
    B. Adventurers, tourists, and travelers
    C. The changing face of tourism
    D. Tourism: Its advantages and disadvantages

112. What is mentioned about the World Tourism Organization (WTO)?
    A. The WTO has predicted difficulties in controlling the demand for tourism in the twenty-first century.
    B. The WTO was once unequivocally in support of tourism.
    C. The WTO promotes tourism because it is a large part of the world economy.
    D. The WTO is reluctant for the government to get involved.

113. Which of the following best explains the word **clandestine**?
    A. secret
    B. forbidden
    C. negative
    D. illicit

114. Why does the author mention "cultural experiences," "expeditions," or "projects" in paragraph 4 of the passage?
    A. to exemplify how tourists respect the environment
    B. to contradict the evidence in support of advertising
    C. to illustrate how tourism has been re-branded
    D. to argue that charitable expeditions are now indistinguishable from vacations

115. According to the passage, which one of the following examples best characterizes how tourists can be more respectful of their environments?
    A. by avoiding the local culture
    B. by using unconventional types of lodging arrangements
    C. by viewing the local culture in a negative way
    D. by emphasizing the disadvantages of mass tourism

This passage is about the political system.

Vicissitudes in the political arena are predominant among the events reported in today's press. Stupendous scandals have been uncovered and covert operations foiled as a result of recent media investigations. This may occur after immense and assiduous research into the particular discrepancies among different versions of stories told by a politician or may simply result from an investigative journalist following an instinctive hunch. Had many duplicitous politicians been aware of the menace posed by such journalists, they would have been much more careful in carrying out their subterfuge.

The methods utilized in various scandals and subsequent cover-ups may include secret surveillance of governmental offices, telephone hacking, or purging relevant data from computer systems. It is not surprising that many people would consider such perfidy towards the democratic process as tantamount to espionage or treason.

Once a scandal is uncovered, the politician will be subjected to questioning at a public hearing. Most politicians do not respond with complete candor during these proceedings. However, their testimony is irrevocable and cannot be taken back without committing the act of perjury, or lying under oath. Certain politicians may phlegmatically profess no knowledge of the matter under investigation, while others may claim that their recollection of the events is unclear, but most parties involved will attempt to reply to questioning deftly and resolutely with cogent arguments and apposite remarks.

Ultimately, the hearing is likely to have an adverse impact on the politician's career. During the hearing, the politician may be subjected to daily jeering from throngs of spectators assembled outside the hearing room. The politician may even be forced to relinquish his or her position as a consequence of a unanimous consensus, and, thus be banished from public office for the remainder of his or her career.

116. According to the passage, how does the public learn about political scandals?
    A. They can come to light because of similar accounts of events.
    B. The public prefers these stories to be covert.
    C. These stories are frequently mentioned in the news.
    D. The politicians want to publicize the stories.

117. The reader can conclude that disloyal politicians may attempt to do which of the following?
    A. eliminate incriminating digital media
    B. commit perfidy to avoid responsibility
    C. exercise more caution in their affairs subsequent to giving up public office
    D. respond candidly to interrogation

118. What do most politicians do during public hearings?
    A. answer questions frankly and with clarity
    B. hesitate slightly before responding
    C. recall events accurately
    D. try to reply with appropriate statements

119. What is mentioned about the public hearing?
    A. It may result in the exile of the politician to another country.
    B. It may expose the politician to public ridicule.
    C. It is poorly attended by members of the public.
    D. Researchers are not allowed to attend it.

120. Which statement best expresses the main idea of the passage?
    A. The political arena in this day and age is extremely fluid.
    B. The public hearing may result in the demise of the politician's career.
    C. Most politicians are hiding some sort of scandal.
    D. Most parties reply hesitantly to questions at the public hearing.

ECPE
PRACTICE TEST 1
ANSWER KEY

1. C
2. A
3. C
4. C
5. A
6. C
7. D
8. A
9. D
10. B
11. B
12. A
13. B
14. A
15. C
16. A
17. A
18. C
19. B
20. B
21. B
22. C
23. D
24. B
25. A
26. D
27. B
28. C

29. D
30. D
31. C
32. B
33. C
34. A
35. D
36. B
37. C
38. D
39. A
40. A
41. A
42. C
43. D
44. B
45. C
46. D
47. C
48. B
49. A
50. B
51. B
52. D
53. B
54. D
55. A
56. C
57. B
58. A
59. C
60. B

61. D
62. B
63. C
64. C
65. A
66. D
67. A
68. A
69. D
70. C
71. B
72. A
73. C
74. B
75. D
76. C
77. C
78. B
79. A
80. D
81. C
82. D
83. A
84. B
85. C
86. D
87. B
88. A
89. C
90. D
91. B
92. B

93. D
94. C
95. C
96. A
97. C
98. C
99. C
100. A
101. B
102. A
103. C
104. C
105. B
106. D
107. D
108. D
109. C
110. B
111. C
112. D
113. B
114. B
115. D
116. A
117. D
118. D
119. C
120. A

ECPE
PRACTICE TEST 2
ANSWER KEY

1. D
2. A
3. D
4. D
5. B
6. B
7. A
8. C
9. B
10. C
11. B
12. C
13. C
14. B
15. A
16. B
17. C
18. C
19. C
20. A
21. C
22. D
23. B
24. B
25. B
26. D
27. C
28. C

29. B
30. B
31. A
32. D
33. D
34. A
35. C
36. D
37. B
38. C
39. A
40. B
41. A
42. B
43. D
44. B
45. C
46. D
47. C
48. B
49. C
50. C
51. A
52. C
53. C
54. A
55. A
56. B
57. C
58. D
59. D
60. B

61. D
62. A
63. C
64. C
65. D
66. C
67. D
68. A
69. B
70. B
71. D
72. C
73. A
74. D
75. A
76. C
77. A
78. D
79. D
80. C
81. B
82. A
83. A
84. B
85. C
86. D
87. C
88. A
89. D
90. C
91. C
92. B

93. C
94. B
95. C
96. B
97. A
98. C
99. A
100. D
101. A
102. B
103. A
104. D
105. C
106. A
107. B
108. D
109. B
110. C
111. D
112. C
113. D
114. A
115. B
116. D
117. A
118. A
119. C
120. B

ECPE
PRACTICE TEST 3
ANSWER KEY

1. D
2. C
3. C
4. C
5. C
6. D
7. B
8. B
9. C
10. B
11. A
12. B
13. D
14. B
15. C
16. A
17. D
18. A
19. C
20. D
21. C
22. C
23. C
24. A
25. D
26. A
27. B
28. B

29. A
30. C
31. B
32. A
33. C
34. B
35. C
36. C
37. B
38. B
39. B
40. B
41. B
42. C
43. B
44. B
45. D
46. B
47. D
48. C
49. A
50. D
51. A
52. C
53. B
54. B
55. A
56. D
57. B
58. A
59. B
60. C

61. B
62. C
63. D
64. A
65. A
66. C
67. D
68. A
69. B
70. B
71. A
72. B
73. D
74. C
75. A
76. B
77. B
78. A
79. B
80. D
81. B
82. A
83. D
84. C
85. A
86. D
87. D
88. B
89. A
90. A
91. B
92. A

93. C
94. D
95. A
96. C
97. C
98. B
99. A
100. D
101. A
102. A
103. B
104. C
105. C
106. A
107. C
108. B
109. A
110. A
111. B
112. A
113. A
114. C
115. C
116. A
117. A
118. A
119. D
120. D

ECPE
PRACTICE TEST 4
ANSWER KEY

1. A
2. A
3. B
4. D
5. C
6. B
7. A
8. B
9. B
10. A
11. A
12. C
13. D
14. A
15. C
16. B
17. A
18. A
19. B
20. C
21. D
22. B
23. A
24. B
25. C
26. A
27. B
28. B

29. C
30. B
31. A
32. A
33. B
34. C
35. A
36. C
37. A
38. C
39. B
40. A
41. C
42. D
43. A
44. D
45. C
46. C
47. A
48. C
49. D
50. A
51. C
52. A
53. B
54. C
55. A
56. B
57. C
58. C
59. B
60. C

61. B
62. A
63. D
64. A
65. C
66. C
67. D
68. D
69. B
70. D
71. B
72. B
73. A
74. D
75. A
76. C
77. B
78. A
79. D
80. C
81. C
82. B
83. A
84. D
85. D
86. B
87. C
88. A
89. A
90. B
91. C
92. A

93. D
94. B
95. A
96. D
97. A
98. D
99. C
100. B
101. C
102. A
103. C
104. B
105. D
106. B
107. C
108. D
109. C
110. D
111. C
112. A
113. A
114. C
115. B
116. C
117. A
118. D
119. B
120. A

www.ingramcontent.com/pod-product-compliance
Lightning Source LLC
Chambersburg PA
CBHW081750100526
44592CB00015B/2363